IMAGES OF

HULL

IMAGES OF
HULL

compiled by Barbara Power

bringing people *together*
for the **Millennium**

Breedon Books
Publishing Company
Derby

First published in Great Britain by
The Breedon Books Publishing Company Limited
Breedon House, 44 Friar Gate, Derby, DE1 1DA.
1999

ISBN 1 85983 147 8

Printed and bound by Butler & Tanner Ltd., Selwood Printing Works,
Caxton Road, Frome, Somerset.

Colour separations by GreenShires Ltd, Leicester.

Jackets printed by Lawrence-Allen, Avon.

Contents

Introduction

The *Hull Daily Mail* is more than a newspaper… it is a way of life!

For more than a century it has recorded, in words and pictures, the daily events in the area – the triumphs and failures, achievements and disasters. It has informed, entertained and, when necessary, campaigned vigorously on behalf of its readers.

Pages of job vacancies, of cars and houses for sale, shopping bargains, family announcements and classified advertisements – all of which add up to a vital service for Hull and East Yorkshire.

The *Mail* began life in 1787 when the *Hull Packet*, comprising four pages, was established. It continued until 1887 when the *Hull Daily Mail* published its first edition on 29 September from offices in Whitefriargate.

Like the *Mail* today, the first issue was a collection of local, national and international news and sport.

The *Mail* moved to purpose-built premises in Jameson Street in 1926. Those offices served us well, seeing us safely through World War Two and the many changes that went on around us.

Now we are established at Blundell's Corner with the latest in technology to help us meet the challenges of the next century.

Words for our pages are now produced with the aid of computers in place of our dear friend, the typewriter, and pictorial images can be transmitted digitally and with the aid of satellites.

In *Images of Hull* we have the opportunity to revisit some of the early photographs taken to illustrate and capture moments of time in the city's history.

These pictures have been used throughout the decades in the *Hull Daily Mail* and, as the new Millennium dawns, provide an amazing record of life in the 20th century.

Together these images produce a fascinating glimpse of the charm and character of Hull that still endures.

Stan Szecowka
Community and Campaigns
Editor
Hull Daily Mail

The *Hull Daily Mail's* fleet of delivery vans, all lined up during World War One. One of the placards on the vans tells: 'Loss of Hull Steamer and Four Lives'.

Life at a Slower Pace

Small children play around Hull's famous Fisherman's statue in the early years of the 20th century while some of the city's older residents use the same location to sit awhile and chat about old times.

Hull Market Place in 1887. The photograph shows the section of the street which was destroyed by German bombs in World War Two.

Two Hull electric trams travel up Carr Lane towards Victoria Square. The horse and cart driver take the opportunity to ride along the tram path which carried public transport the other way.

'S' trams on Spring Bank in 1901. It is either a spring or autumn day as the trees are not in full leaf, although the ivy climbing up the house in the right of the picture is abundant.

Another view of Spring Bank in 1901 as two men and a woman cycle down the road in the wake of yet another tram.

This triumphal arch was erected in Whitefriargate for the visit of the Prince and Princess of Wales in 1903.

Victoria Square in 1911 with Edwardian fashions still evident. The tall building on the left, the Prudential Assurance Building, was destroyed in a German air-raid in May 1941. On the right are buildings, which include Powolny's, which were in King Edward Street.

These elegantly-dressed ladies are walking on Victoria Square in 1911. A small child is given a lift on a horse and cart.

Bicycles are the most evident form of transport on Monument Bridge in Hull's city centre between the wars.

A newspaper seller is engrossed in the day's news while tending his pitch outside the Midland Bank in Silver Street in the 1930s. One placard reads: 'Prison Murder Scandal'. Another appears to say: 'Charlie Chaplin by Winston Churchill'. Presumably there must have been more to it than that!

Hull Co-operative Society's store at the corner of Jameson Street about 1939. The white-coated policeman is giving signals although there is little or no traffic to be seen.

Old trams and yesterday's styles near North Bridge in the 1930s. The clock says midday. Crowds gather on both pavements and the bridge is decked out with flags and bunting, presumably for a royal occasion.

This lady takes a second glance at the horse and cart tethered outside solicitors' offices in Parliament Street between the wars.

The Hull Savings Bank at the corner of Smeaton Street and George Street, pictured probably in the late 1950s or early '60s.

Life *had* to be at a slower pace in the Land of Green Ginger in October 1954 when the River Hull overflowed its banks and flooded areas of the old town. A No Parking sign sits helpfully on the water's edge.

Susanna's Terrace, Bean Street, in the early 1960s. Children play and a mother and daughter use the family pushchair to move some possessions.

The horse wash at Hull Corporation Pier on a summer's day in the 1950s.

There were always some people who had time to stand and watch when small boats or barges took on cargo at Hull Corporation Pier.

Almost as good as a day at the seaside – Hull Corporation Pier in 1949. The river is busy but most people want to read their newspaper, eat their sandwiches, or just pass the time of day with their neighbour.

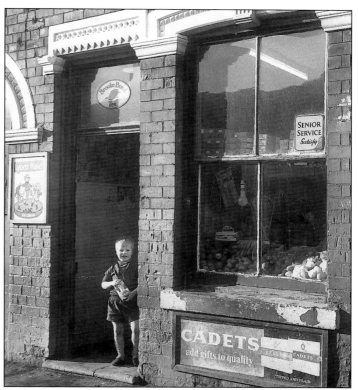

The butcher's shop of John M. Taylor of 24 Witham, Hull, between the wars. The Witham was a busy Hull shopping street and a 1929 trade directory has Mr Taylor's shop flanked by a confectioner's and a clothes shop. Just up the road was a famous old name – the Home and Colonial.

This retail outlet operated from a house in West Parade, Spring Bank. The window is full of fruit and vegetables and they also sold ice-cream and cigarettes. The small boy in the doorway holds a packet of Golden Wonder crisps priced at 3p, so the photograph must have been taken after decimalisation in 1971. The shop had closed by 1977.

The window display at Waterloo Street sub-Post Office attracted plenty of young window-shoppers, probably because it was mostly full of toys and sporting equipment. Note the Victorian post box.

Landmarks

An artist's impression of one of Hull's most significant buildings, the Public Rooms, which were replaced by the New Theatre after the turn of the century.

The statue of King William looks up at the tower of Holy Trinity Church in the Market Place.

This photograph shows the old Grammar School on South Churchside. A great deal of money had been spent on refurbishing the interior of the 15th-century school premises but in 1977 Hull Civic Society were still unhappy that market stalls were still allowed to obscure the dignified frontage from the visitor's view.

The Hull birthplace, in the High Street, of the great emancipator of slaves, William Wilberforce. The 12ft statue atop a 90ft column was erected by public subscription in 1834, following his death and contemporary with the final abolition of slavery in the British colonies. The statue originally stood on Monument Bridge and was moved to this site in the 1930s. Wilberforce House later became the College of Further Education. This photograph was taken in January 1932.

Hull's historic Charterhouse and a closer view of the commemorative mosaic on its steps.

Hull Trinity House, in Trinity House Lane, the home of the self-financing charity, The Corporation of the Hull Trinity House which is now 630 years old.

Hull Royal Infirmary pictured in 1952. Today it is the entrance to Hull's Prospect Centre.

Fountain in Park Avenue, pictured on a wet day in the early 1930s.

The entrance to one of Hull's oldest public houses, Ye Olde White Harte, a 17th-century building where in April 1642, the Mayor, Henry Bernard, the local MP, Peregrine Pelham, and the Governor of Hull, Sir John Hotham, met and decided to keep the gates to the city closed to King Charles I.

A later view of one of the fountains in the Avenues area of Hull.

The monument erected in Spring Bank cemetery to victims of cholera.

The Stoneferry bandstand pictured before World War Two.

Hepworth's Arcade in Hull, showing the handsome roof. This photograph was taken in 1975.

Transports of Delight

Members of a Hull cycling club outside the Manchester Hotel in 1899. The main attraction seems to be the remarkable five-seater cycle. Hull was always a popular centre for cycling, with several clubs operating over the years.

In 1962 these gentleman on a cycling holiday found time to visit Hull Transport Museum in High Street to examine machines of 100 years earlier.

Trams from the horse-drawn days in Hull. One vehicle is decorated and a man in uniform – perhaps an old soldier? – stands by the rear stairway. The other tram is going to Holderness Road and Savile Street.

Electric trams come to Hull. Civic dignitaries ride on top and crowds throng the flag-bedecked street as this tram from Anlaby Road and St John Street heads for the city centre.

Two of Hull's first tickets for electric trams. Ticket 3535 was the first to be issued on the electric tram from Savile Street to Botanic Gardens. Ticket 3636 was the first to be issued for an electric tram journey in the opposite direction. Advertised on the back is the 'Yuos' cure for gout and rheumatism, sold by Power and Ricardo of George Street, Hull.

A 'military tram' of Hull Tramways Department, photographed just after the outbreak of World War One in 1914.

Driver and conductress pose at the door of their 'D' route Hull tram while a well-dressed woman looks back at the camera.

Miss Annie Winter was one of many women employed as conductresses by Hull Tramways from 1915 onwards as men employees went off to war.

Trams at the Anlaby Road depot. They are all of the 'A' route. The destination board of the vehicle on the left says 'Alexandra Dock'.

An Anlaby Road trolley bus photographed in June 1959.

A Hull trolley bus on a route via Beverley Road waits for pedestrians to cross in Victoria Square in the late 1950s.

April showers meant that day turned to night in Hull when this picture was taken on Budget Day 1958. There was a strong wind accompanied by heavy rain, according to the original caption.

The last-ever Hull trolley bus on the 64 route, pictured on 21 September 1963.

In this photograph the 64 route is now served by a petrol-driven bus. It is travelling under North Bridge.

The *Mail* had photographs of the wedding of the Duke of Kent and Princess Marina of Greece and Denmark in 1934 flown from London. They were picked up by delivery van at the local airport.

To mark the coronation of Queen Elizabeth II in June 1953, the *Hull Daily Mail* dressed up their delivery vans. This one delivered copies of the newspaper to shops in Goole.

Botanic Gardens Station in 1952 as Hull mothers and their children get ready to board a train for Witherensea.

Built at the beginning of World War Two, this War Department steam engine was still doing a fine job in the Hull area in the early 1960s.

Botanic Gardens Station was unusually busy when this photograph was taken in the 1940s. Sunday excursion trains returning to Hull were stopped there due to the closure of Paragon Station for the relaying of intersection track to the approaches to the platform. Normal traffic terminated at Hull Stepney, except trains from Scarborough which stopped at Cottingham.

The sign says 'No Waiting' but these motorists have no option as they queue up at the Dairycoates level-crossing in June 1959.

Hull children watch a train going over an unattended level-crossing in February 1962. Minutes later they were snowballing in the middle of the track.

New gates, the first of their type in Hull, were installed at the Walton Street level-crossing in December 1963.

It's days are numbered. A Friday evening in July 1964 and the Anlaby Road level-crossing gates are closed for the last time. In future, pedestrians would use a footbridge, vehicles a flyover.

February 1965 and trackmen regrade ballast between the railway lines on what used to be the Anlaby Road level-crossing. The level-crossing lines removed and ordinary lines substituted.

Platelayers stand back as a train passes Snuff Mill Lane level-crossing in June 1964.

In August 1956 this diesel train went from Hull to Gristhorpe on an experimental run. The driver was Mr J. Sewell of Hull.

On a late spring day in 1966 this loco bites into the incline over Dairycoates sidings. It is the 8.25am from Hull Paragon to Doncaster, the last steam-hauled passenger train operating out of Hull. Soon it would be replaced by a diesel unit.

Loco engineer Chris Malyon chats with driver Alf Wisker and stoker Alan Hazel, who are aboard this King Arthur Class locomotive in March 1982. It had been restored to its former glory by members of the Humberside Locomotive Preservation Group and was about to leave Dairycoates depot for a test run to Scarborough.

British Rail driver John Hart enjoyed a 'busman's holiday' in December 1985 when he took the *Alderman Draper* 'Santa Special' to Scarborough and back.

Young man astride his BSA 250 Star, watched by an admiring young lady, in May 1965. Apparently this was the tuned Sports Star (SS80) 'for the more experienced rider', according to the original caption.

Fashions and modes of transport have changed a great deal since this photograph of a young lady and a Vespa 90 motor scooter was taken in the 1960s.

And finally… driving in Hull became a little easier in September 1962 when the flyover bridge at Dairycoates was opened. Here the Lord Mayor's car – 'KH1' – marks the opening of a single carriageway of the flyover.

The Docklands

Kingston upon Hull was once renowned as Britain's 'third port'. It had full accommodation for the quick and economical handling of goods to and from all parts of the world. Connections by road, rail and water from Hull to the whole industrial area were excellent.

Hull once had 11 docks and 13 miles of quays. Riverside quays provided facilities for the discharge and loading of chemicals in bulk.

With the demise of much industry in Hull, some of the city's docks have been redeveloped into such things as a marina, leisure gardens and housing.

Albert Dock

Albert Dock opened in 1869 and was shared between the fishing industry and local merchants until the St Andrew's Dock was opened. It was joined in 1910 by the William Wright Dock. Albert Dock closed to commercial shipping in 1972 but the fishing industry was transferred back there in 1975.

Following the removal of the Albert Dock lock gates in September 1953, workmen repair sills beneath the water with the aid of a cassiow.

In December 1957 workmen began to replace the Riverside Quay which stretched the length of Albert Dock and which was damaged in the wartime blitz on the city.

April 1957 and the first pile is driven in the bed of the Albert Dock during the Riverside Quay and Albert Dock reconstruction scheme. The pile was 70ft long and was of a pre-stressed hollow reinforced design. Construction engineers had to design a cantilever mobile piling gantry made of Bailey bridging material.

August 1958 and rows of tractors at Albert Dock await shipment to overseas markets.

In October 1967, three ships of the Polish Ocean Lines Gdynia-UK service were pictured in Albert Dock. The new *Jaslo*, in Hull for the first time, lies astern of the *Wolin* and *Koszalin*, with rivercraft nestling under her bows.

Hustle and bustle as the *Borodino* is unloaded at Albert Dock in September 1961.

The view from the William Wright Dock looking towards Albert Dock in August 1969.

Tide time in Albert Dock at the end of an October day in 1969.

Hull bobbers use the automatic discharging machine on the trawler *C. S. Forester* at the Albert Dock.

As part of the Hull Fish Dock reorganisation scheme, involving the transfer to the Albert and William Wright Dock, the lock gates were completely overhauled and are pictured here in September 1975. Some 80ft wide and 35ft deep, they were expected to be put back into place later that month.

Albert Dock moved closer to its new role as the port's Fish Dock in October 1975 when the two repaired outer lock gates, each weighing 100 tons, were lifted into place. This photograph shows the difficult manoeuvre of moving one of the massive gates into position through the water of the dock.

A many-masted scene looking out over Albert Dock, now the new Fish Dock, in August 1978 when much of the local fishing fleet was lying in harbour.

January 1989 and the first jib of the three cranes which were being dismantled on Albert Dock – the Fish Dock – is lowered to the ground.

William Wright Dock

William Wright Dock was opened in 1873 and joined to Albert Dock in 1910. It also closed to commercial shipping in 1972 but, refurbished with Albert Dock, it reopened in 1975 to serve the fishing industry.

William Wright Dock pictured in 1901 when the masts of sailing ships filled the horizon.

June 1965 and no cranes were working on William Wright Dock because Hull dockers there had stopped work.

January 1967 and ammunition barges unload 250 tons of ammunition at William Wright Dock. The ammunition was from USAF bases in France. Firemen stand by as a precaution.

Alexandra Dock

Alexandra Dock opened in 1885 and served larger cargo vessels. It closed to commercial shipping in 1982 but reopened in 1991.

August 1949 and two Hull lightermen take a well-earned breather on the hatch cover of a cargo of hides awaiting shipment from Alexandra Dock to Poland.

Picketing at Alexandra Dock in November 1957 when all dockers ceased work in a dispute over a Panamanian-registered vessel.

Busy scene at Alexandra Dock in May 1958.

Two tons to spare as the Alexandra Dock steam crane, capable of lifting 100 tons, swings a 98-ton extractor unit on to the MV *Sertan*.

Not from Mars – these cranes at Alexandra Dock certainly had a futuristic look when this photograph was taken in June 1962.

Cargo from many lands being unloaded at Alexandra Dock in March 1968.

Cars and tractors awaiting export from Hull's Alexandra Dock in July 1968.

Lorry loads of timber at Alexandra Dock in 1968.

Timber unloading at Alexandra Dock in 1972.

More tractors for export at Alexandra Dock, this time in January 1970.

This is part of a record cargo of onions for Hull, unloaded at Alexandra Dock from the Russian ship the 3,100-ton *Parkhomenko* in March 1973. The vessel carried 90,000 bags of onions. Some 72,000 bags (1,780 tons) were unloaded before the *Parkhomenko* left for Rotterdam.

Queen's Dock

The first of all Hull's dock system became known as Queen's Dock in 1854 and closed 1930. It was subsequently filled in and became Queen's Gardens in 1935.

Artist's impression of what became known as Queen's Dock, shortly after its original opening in 1778.

Photograph of Queen's Dock around the turn of the century.

Another view of Queen's Dock, this time during the early years of the 20th century.

Keels and steam trawlers pictured at Queen's Dock around the turn of the century.

Queen's Dock pictured in 1926.

The filling-in of Queen's Dock in 1930, when it was closed.

Queen's Dock in 1930, showing its location in relation to the city centre and the Guildhall.

An aerial view of Queen's Dock in 1930.

Humber Dock

Humber Dock was opened in 1809, the second dock in Hull's dock system. It closed to shipping in 1969 and is now Hull Marina.

A horse and cart driver and some children watch the sluice at the entrance to Humber Dock getting its periodic clean-out in August 1949. Small culverts were opened in the dock gates and the water which rushed through cleared away the mud which had collected.

Fireman battle the fire at Humber Dock in July 1951.

Cutting a new corner to replace a damaged dock face at Humber Dock in March 1949.

The aftermath of the July 1951 fire at Humber Dock.

Two schoolchildren on their
Easter holiday in 1949 watch
firemen cleaning the fireboat at Humber Dock.

The Little Bridge on
Humber Dock, pictured in
January 1962. The original
caption said: 'Only the
modern car on the bridge,
which divides Prince's Dock
and Humber Dock, gives a
date to this unchanging
view.'

Pleasure craft and barges from Prince's Dock and Railway Dock are berthed at Humber Dock in October 1968.

On the eve of Humber Dock's closure in July 1969, lock gateman D. Bennett looks at a bollard made from a cannon barrel and ball from the old waterfront defences. Moored to it is the last vessel to leave the dock, on board which Sir Winston Churchill conferred with naval chiefs at Scapa Flow during World War Two.

Contrasts in Humber Dock basin in August 1978, an immaculate yacht and a not-so-ship-shape barge stuck in the mud.

Lowering a diving bell into Humber Dock, near the old dock gates, to obtain core samples in January 1981.

With the water in Humber Dock held back by piling, work on preparing the site for the hanging of the new lock gates for the proposed Marina in June 1981.

Railway Dock

Railway Dock opened in 1846, the fourth of Hull's town docks system. In 1968 it closed to commercial shipping and is now an annex of the Marina.

Railway Dock pictured in 1901.

The busy Railway Dock around the beginning of the 20th century.

Youngster alone with his thoughts at Railway Dock in January 1969.

An aerial view of Railway Dock in 1978.

This salvaged barge in Railway Dock had been submerged in mud and water for 15 years when it was moved in November 1982 because it was in the way of dredging work so that Railway Dock could form part of the new Marina.

Prince's Dock

In 1854, Junction Dock was renamed Prince's Dock after the Prince Consort, Albert, the husband of Queen Victoria. Junction Dock had first opened in 1829.

Prince's Dock, a hive of industry when this photograph was taken around the turn of the century.

Prince's Dock pictured in March 1948.

Prince's Dock looking towards Hull city centre in 1955.

The same view of Prince's Dock in August 1958 with minesweepers, trawlers, tugs and barges set against a backdrop of the Dock Offices and City Hall.

The old Prince's Dock bonded warehouse was designed by John Bernard Hartley in the 1840s and was one of the first fireproof warehouses in the UK. In 1969 it was said to be unsafe in parts but Hull Civic Society were among those who hoped it could be reprieved from demolition.

A summer's day spent swimming amidst the ships at Prince's Dock in the 1950s.

In 1976 these anglers, complete with umbrellas, test the water at Prince's Dock in a Sunday morning scene.

Pleasure craft were using Prince's Dock when this photograph was taken in 1969.

Looking south over Prince's Dock in May 1979 – and not a sailing vessel in sight.

Victoria Dock

Victoria Dock opened in 1850 and was, for many years, the centre of the timber-importing trade in Hull. It closed in 1970 and has since been filled in and is now the site of a housing development.

View from Victoria Pier on to Victoria Dock in December 1949.

The five-masted barque *Carl Vinnen* unloading timber at Victoria Dock in July 1937.

Dockers busy at Victoria Dock unloading timber from a Swedish vessel in October 1949.

More timber being unloaded at Victoria Dock in 1949.

This time it is the Norwegian timber ship *Finse* being unloaded at Victoria Dock in September 1960.

In 1964, heavy imports of timber caused a shortage of railway wagons and over 20 ships were waiting in the river for discharge. These ships have made it as far as Victoria Dock.

August 1969 and small boats find a temporary haven in Victoria Dock.

Boat owners hold discussions in a quiet corner of Victoria Dock in January 1970.

The setting sun brings a sparkle to well-worn cobbles at Victoria Dock in July 1976.

Filling in Victoria Dock for the Hull River Bridge and South Dock Road scheme in August 1977.

King George Dock

King George Dock was opened in 1914 by King George V, just in time for the outbreak of World War One.

Local dignatories photographed at the opening of King George Dock in 1914.

The SS *Aida* from Port Harcourt, Nigeria, unloading seed into barges at King George Dock in August 1949.

A small boy and an adult watch the *Uskport* being unloaded at King George Dock after World War Two.

The *Consuelo* moored at King George Dock in September 1961.

Work in progress on the North Quay at King George Dock in January 1962.

The new North Quay at King George Dock pictured in September 1964.

Construction work under way at King George Dock in August 1962.

Work on a culvert at King George Dock in August 1963. When completed it would raise the level of water in the dock to allow ships to enter at any state of tide. It was the last stage of a £4.75 million dock improvement scheme.

August 1963 and thousands of pit props from Russia are stacked on King George Dock. This job being carried out by Hull dockers was called 'teaming a cargo'.

A cargo of cars for export to America lies strike-bound at King George Dock in June 1966. One ship they would not sail on was the *Norwave*, in the background, from the roll-on-roll-off service and one of the first ships to suffer from the seamen's strike.

Happier times. The roll-on-roll-off ferries *Svea* (left) and *Norwave* taking on their cargoes for Scandinavia at King George Dock in July 1968. Behind the vessels is a grain silo.

Queen Elizabeth Dock

Work on a 28-acre extension to the 1914 King George Dock was started in 1969 and eventually the new Queen Elizabeth Dock cost £6,750,000. It was opened by Queen Elizabeth II in 1969.

June 1971 and the new 40-ton container transporter crane at Queen Elizabeth Dock. It was due to come into service a few weeks later.

One of five giant carriers for the new Queen Elizabeth Dock, pictured in October 1970. The men who would drive them at the new container terminal would be working 20ft above the ground.

March 1973 and the new roll-on-roll-off terminal at Queen Elizabeth Dock is open for business. The occasion was marked with a reception aboard MV *Hero*, the first vessel to use the facility.

When the Queen opened Queen Elizabeth Dock in 1969 she unveiled a polished aluminium plaque to commemorate the occasion. The ceremony took place in a quayside shed but the Queen asked that the plaque be given a permanent home. In May 1972 this was done when it was resited, set in a plinth of Lakeland green stone which carried a concrete bracket supporting the beam bearing the name of the dock.

Lorry leaving Queen Elizabeth Dock in September 1975.

By May 1976 this double roll-on-roll-off ramp was no longer in use at Queen Elizabeth Dock.

The Humber-based tug *Lady Moira* brings a giant 160ft-high, 480-tonnes crane to Queen Elizabeth Dock in April 1978. It was towed the 640 miles from Newport, South Wales, where it was built. When the crane was eventually modified and brought into use, Queen Elizabeth Dock would have greatly increased capacity.

A busy scene on Queen Elizabeth Dock in the late 1970s.

Unloading the *Cedarbank* at Queen Elizabeth Dock in September 1982. The cargo was clearly one to be respected.

Fishing out of Hull

In the first half of the 20th century Hull was the greatest deep-sea trawling port in the world and for many local people there was no other life outside of Hessle Road, right near the Fish Dock, as it was the home of the fishermen of Hull and their families.

In 1961, Hull's first stern trawler, part-fresher, part-freezer, the *Lord Nelson*, was introduced, followed a year later by the *Junella*, the port's first all-freezer stern trawler.

In 1975, the imposition by Iceland of the 200-mile fishing limit meant that the Hull fleet was totally dependent on the deep-sea fishing industry and as a result of the restrictions, most of the stern trawlers found that they had, quite literally, nowhere to fish. Many were sold, others scrapped.

By the 1970s, many men had been made redundant and thus began the decline of Hull's once-great fishing industry and the Hessle Road development began to break up with the population being transferred to other council estates.

St Andrew's Docks, which served as the Fish Dock after Albert Dock became used exclusively for commercial shipping, is now closed and has been redeveloped. Fishing was transferred back to Albert Dock in 1975.

Hull's 'dream trawler' puts to sea in August 1957. The 800-ton *Cape Trafalgar* – the fishing industry's second diesel electric trawler – leaves Humber Dock for her trials in the river before joining Hull's fishing fleet.

The *St Wistan* is slowly manoeuvred through St Andrew's Dock in February 1960.

Will Longden watches deckie-learner Terry Crockett pegging up the trawl nets to dry as the *Kingston Amber* steams off the Faroes in September 1958.

The *Junella*, Hull's first all-freezer stern trawler, is launched at Aberdeen in March 1962. She cost an estimated £500,000 to build and fit-out.

A busy scene at St Andrew's Dock in February 1960 as Hull-based trawlers are prepared for their next trip to the fishing grounds.

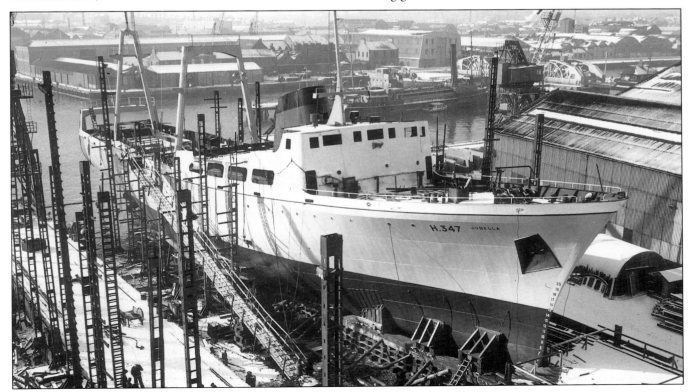

Still waters reflect the troubled scene at St Andrew's Dock in April 1961 during the five-day-old Hull trawler strike.

Home from the fishing grounds, these trawlers are berthed at St Andrew's Dock in April 1962. Some are discharging their catch, others prepare to put to sea again.

Work goes on at St Andrew's Dock in April 1965.

Packed like frozen fish, these giant all-freeze trawlers are moored in a corner of St Andrew's Dock in June 1967.

Heavy seas and a heaving deck aboard a Hull trawler, in November 1972, fishing inside what was then a 50-mile limit imposed by Iceland.

More vessels from Hull's world-famous fishing fleet moored at St Andrew's Dock, this time in August 1967.

Mate Paul Wheeldon (left) at the winch of the trawler *Ross Otranto* off Iceland in January 1976.

Once familiar to Hull's fishermen – the subway sign at St Andrew's Dock, pictured in January 1971.

A terse message in one of the kits of fish landed at Albert Dock in October 1975, when the fishing industry was transferred back there from St Andrew's Dock.

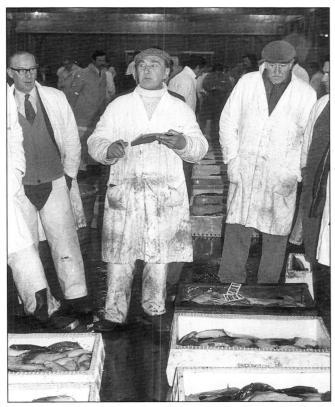

Boxes of fish await distribution at Albert Dock in December 1975.

A catch from the *Lord Nelson* being auctioned at Albert Dock in January 1979.

Mr Clive Ellis, a worker with Ross Fish, contemplates the future at Hull's Albert Dock in September 1984.

The hustle and bustle of Albert Dock with its busy turnaround of trawlers is a thing of the past and taking advantage of the quiet waters for their fishing trip in December 1986 are three Hull lads, Paul Stead, Jonathan Jones and Michael Carlson.

Memories… Bill Taylor revisits Albert Dock in March 1988.

Kingston Communications

Kingston Communications telephone system began in 1911 when private sector telecommunications in Britain were nationalised.

Hull's unique system, established in 1902, was so successful that Kingston upon Hull City Council purchased the local telephone network, despite opposition from the National Telephone Company.

The first civic telephone exchange was opened in the former Trippett's Baths, Wincolmlee, in 1904. The company's system was cared for by the General Post Office in 1912, but two years later the Hull area was sold to the Corporation and the two systems were gradually merged until they were one entity.

From then until 1963, Hull Corporation Telephone Department's head office and central exchange were housed in Mytongate and that same year, Telephone House was opened in Carr Lane.

In 1987, Kingston Communications (Hull) plc took over the running of the city's telecommunications which now serves over 500,000 people in and around Hull.

Hull Telephone Department's first exchange opened here at Wincolmlee in 1904. The former Trippett's Baths and Washhouses, the building was demolished in 1971.

July 1951 and work is being carried out on Hull's automatic exchange – the only civic telephone exchange in the country.

Civic heads visit Hull telephone exchange in December 1953.

Hull's telephone disc jockey in February 1957 is Joyce Robson, who dealt with callers requesting top tunes of the day, with a changed programme every week.

General view of Hull's telephone exchange in August 1957.

Hull telephone exchange in May 1961 when, according to the original caption, there was 'a big wastage' because of marriages'.

In May 1971, a *Hull Daily Mail* photographer took this picture of the teak telephone kiosk outside the Guildhall. The kiosk was about to be removed.

In March 1963, the first wall-telephone – originally issued 60 years earlier – is photographed in use (left) next to the newly-issued wall and table model soon to be available to Hull subscribers. Feature writer Tom Dobney and secretary Josephine Cawkwell posed for the picture.

The manual switchboard at Mytongate Exchange, pictured shortly before its closure in May 1964, when Telephone House in Carr Lane opened.

October 1964 and Telephone House in Carr Lane is fully operational, a far cry from the days at the old Trippett's Baths and Washhouse at Wincolmlee, which had opened some 60 years earlier.

Telephone engineers testing equipment at Carr Lane in October 1964.

Amazing maze: Technicians Phil Wingfield (on ladder) and Eric Garside working on the main distribution frame from where telephone subscribers come into Telephone House, Carr Lane. This picture was taken in April 1976.

May 1974 and different styles of telephone kiosks are pictured side by side on Spring Bank West, Hull. The caption writer wondered how long it would be before the familiar old style (left) with its wrought-iron crowns and squared windows, would become collectors' items.

Dial 999!

Fire

Cottingham Fire Brigade pictured in 1887 with their horse-drawn fire appliance.

In March 1963, this 100-year-old fire engine was receiving a final polish before taking part in a parade.

Pedestrians and traffic, including a Hull Corporation tram, make way for a fire engine in Anlaby Road in the years just after World War One.

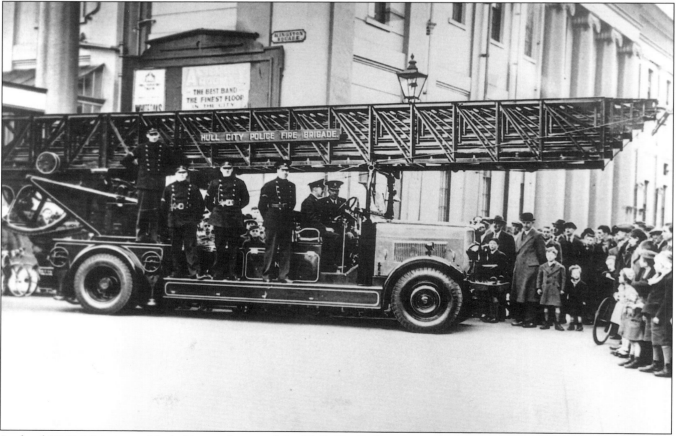

Leyland TML Metz turntable ladder and men of the Hull City Police Fire Brigade on show for the public in Kingston Square between the wars.

Police hold back pedestrians as this Hull fire engine races to a fire in the city around 1925.

Probably unique to Hull was this warning sign which facilitated the passage of the city's fire engines.

Hull's Auxiliary Fire Service practise with their fire float. The AFS played a vital role during the wartime blitz on the city.

August 1963 and the monitor guns fore and aft of this Hull fireboat are demonstrated. They fired 10 tons of water every minute.

Hull's No.1 turntable ladder and its crew, pictured in October 1953.

Hull Fire Brigade's new emergency lighting unit on display in June 1950.

The control room of Hull Central Fire Station in October 1961. This is where all the city's 999 calls were received.

Hull's first white fire appliance on show at the Central Fire Station in April 1970.

Ambulance

A new ambulance for Hull awaits inspection by the Health Committee in April 1951.

In 1955, these ambulances were put on display to show the new livery adopted by the Kingston upon Hull Ambulance Service.

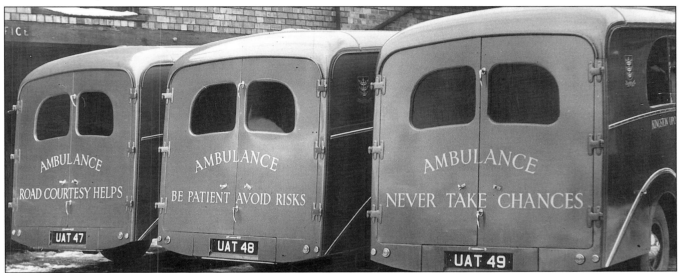

Slogans helped too. In February 1956 these ambulances were pictured in their now familiar blue livery but carrying messages designed to force home the points of road safety.

Perhaps not in keeping with the messages preached in the previous photograph, the original caption for this September 1957 photograph read: 'One hand on the wheel, one hand holding the radio receiver and transmitter – that's the way the modern ambulance driver gets his orders'.

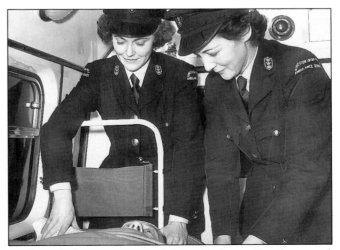

Hull ambulance personnel Mrs Barbara Harrison and Miss Monica Cottrel-Smith needed 'nerves of steel, first-class driving ability, a sound knowledge of first-aid and a sympathetic approach,' according to the notes accompanying this September 1957 photograph.

Drivers L. Pierce and H. Kipling pictured in their Hull ambulance in January 1962.

On duty in the control room of the Central Ambulance Station in Osborne Street in January 1962 were Leading driver Victor Harbord, Station Officer George Clarkson and telephonists Billy Freer and Mavis Bays.

Police

The Alfred Gelder Street Police Station pictured at its corner with Parliament Street.

Hull police officers man the telephones at the Alfred Gelder Street Police Station in March 1950.

Police cars and motorcyclists line up for a *Hull Dail Mail* cameraman in November 1957.

Alderman H. Fairbotham, chairman of the Watch Committee, Mr S. Lawrence, Hull's Chief Constable, and the architect, Mr A. Lazenby, viewing the façade of the new Central Police Station in Queen's Gardens in March 1957.

The control room at the Alfred Gelder Street Police Station was the nerve centre of the old building, just as that in the new Central Police Station would play a crucial role.

Above and right: Hull police horse Wilberforce being ridden by PC Knaggs in October 1959 and by PC Wilson in September 1960, when he was photographed rather artistically by the King William statue in Queen Street.

In February 1960 this Hull police constable was using a police telephone to 'ring-in'. There were no personal radios in those days and officers kept in touch via these distinctive phone 'boxes' dotted around the city.

June 1960 and PC K. Page finds that traffic duty in the centre of Hull can be hot work.

In January 1964, Mr Clifford Wood was busy demolishing a cell in the old police station at Alfred Gelder Street.

A summer's evening in July 1961 and two Hull policewomen are pictured on duty in one of the city's ancient cobbled streets

Stop me and buy one? Well it certainly looks like an ice-cream cart but in fact it was a newly-installed kiosk for point duty in Victoria Square in May 1964. The slightly self-conscious looking policeman is PC T. E. Tuxworth.

Hull Police Cadet Norman Harrison waits for the signal to move off in May 1965.

Line-up of Hull police motor-cyclists who took part in a course at Carnaby Airfield near Bridlington in March 1967.

A white police van on patrol in North Hull in June 1967. The plan was for Hull to soon have squads of 'selected' policemen working in the Eastern and Western Divisions and a fleet of new blue and white 'panda' vans in a scheme aimed at cutting down crime and improving police-public relations.

And here they are. July 1967 and Hull's new 'panda' vans and their drivers line up in Pearson Park.

Checking on current merchandise at Hull Market in May 1986 are PC Jim Wilkinson (right) in an inspector's uniform dated 1836 and PC Merrick Head in a constable's uniform of the same era.

Hull in the Blitz

During World War Two, Hull sustained widespread devastation as the result of 82 German air-raids which killed some 1,200 of its citizens and left 95 per cent of its homes damaged in some way or other. Some of the worst Luftwaffe attacks came in 1941 – particularly on the night of 7-8 May – when the docks and other crowded areas of the city were badly hit.

This householder of 31 Victor Street, Hull, surveys the damage wreaked by an incendiary bomb which landed on his home at 11.13pm on the night of 19 June 1940.

A local shop is one of the badly damaged properties in Goddard Street after a raid on 4 February 1941.

Not much chance of survival here after an Anderson shelter suffered extensive damage in March 1941.

Rescuers at work in Fountain Road in March 1941.

Local children inspect the damage in Grange Street in March 1941.

An entire building in George Street is missing after a direct hit in March 1941 but the buildings either side are still standing.

A soldier gives help to a Hull householder whose home was hit in April 1941. What furniture can be salvaged is stacked outside the damaged house in Ferensway.

April 1941 and here soldiers help to clear up in Rokeby Avenue.

In early May 1941, the Prudential Tower in Hull was still standing after one of the worst air-raids of the war, but the following day is was pulled down in the interests of public safety.

Rescue work in progress at Buckingham Street in May 1941.

Costello's Corner, at the junction of Jameson Street and Saville Street, ablaze in May 1941. The statue of Andrew Marvell stands defiantly amid the wreckage of one of Hull's best-known streets.

Bomb damage to the interior of the City Hall in May 1941.

A few days later and the scene in Jameson Street where the Co-op Building had once proudly stood in one of the city's busiest shopping throughfares. Now, in May 1941, the building is but a ruined shell.

What was left of the YWCA headquarters in Prospect Street after the May 1941 raid.

It was once someone's home; now it is a mound of rubble. Durham Street in May 1941.

In July 1941, the Head Post Office in Alfred Gelder Street was wrecked by a German bomb.

All that was left of the safes at the Savings Bank in Holderness Road after a raid in July 1941.

Also in a raid in July 1941, the premises of Reckitt and Coleman in Dansom Lane was partially demolished.

It's hard to imagine what to do next as these officials examine bomb damage in Cottingham Road in 1941.

All that was left of buildings in King Edward Street after a raid in 1941.

'We're not downhearted!' seems to be the message as Union Flags fly over a bombed house in James Reckitt Avenue in 1941.

Radbourne Street – or at least what was left of this part of it – after a 1941 raid on Hull. It was the worst year of a terrible war for the citizens.

Like the buildings around them, these cars parked in Lombard Street, Ferensway, in 1941 look to be write-offs.

Rescuers sift among the ruins of houses in De la Pole Avenue in February 1942.

Not surprisingly, military personnel and a civilian passer-by eye this unexploded bomb with caution in an East Hull street in 1942.

A giant vacuum cleaner used to suck up plaster and other dust after an air-raid on Hull in June 1943.

A huge lump of concrete lies embedded in Bricknell Avenue in 1942.

Hammond's Store, or what remains of it, in Jameson Street in August 1942.

A young boy helps firemen in Caroline Street in June 1943.

An aerial view of Hull's Dansom Lane area after the 1941 blitz on the city.

City Square and King Edward Street in 1946. Peace is restored but the scars of war will take a long time to heal, for Hull was one of the worst-bombed British cities of World War Two.

Royal Visitors

The Prince of Wales, later King Edward VIII and then the Duke of Windsor after he abdicated, on a visit to Hull in 1926. He is seen here at the Craven Park rugby league ground with the Lord Mayor of Hull (Frank Finn) and Mr E. Brown, the chairman of Hull Kingston Rovers FC.

The Prince of Wales' visit to Hull, on 13 October 1926.

King George VI and Queen Elizabeth on a visit to Hull Boys' Club on 19 October 1937.

Following the 1941 blitzes on Hull, King George VI and Queen Elizabeth revisited the city. Here the King and Queen are accompanied by the Sheriff of Hull, Mr R. G. Tarran, and the Lord Mayor (Alderman S. H. Smith).

Queen Elizabeth chatting to Lady Atkinson and the matron of Hull Royal Infirmary, Miss P. Watson.

The King and Queen meet Mr D. E. Crickmay (left) and the Sheriff of Hull, Mr R. G. Tarran.

The King and Queen congratulate members of the rescue services whose courage was tested to the full during heavy German air-raids on the city.

The Queen chats with some of the bombed-out people of Hull.

The Duchess of Kent meets the Lord Mayor of Hull during her visit to the city in April 1943.

The Duchess of Gloucester on her visit to Hull on 8 May 1943.

The Duke of Edinburgh leaves the Guildhall in Alfred Gelder Street on his visit to Hull on 1 December 1948.

The Duke of Edinburgh during his inspection of the trawler *Princess Elizabeth*.

In April 1956 the Duke of Edinburgh returned to Hull to re-open the new building of Hull Trinity House Navigation School.

The Duke inspecting Trinity House boys in April 1956.

Woman workers cheer the Duke as he leaves a Hull factory.

Official luncheon group at the Guildhall during the visit of Queen Elizabeth II and Prince Philip, Duke of Edinburgh, on 18 May 1957. The Lord Mayor and Lady Mayoress are seated to the right.

There is a military guard of honour for the Queen and Prince Philip as they emerge from the Royal Station Hotel.

The Queen is escorted by the Chief Docks Manager, Mr Harold L. Hopkins, as she tours the King George Dock.

Dockers wives and children had a good view of the royal party as they walked along the reconstructed quay at King George Dock.

The Queen shakes hands with charge nurse Mr James E. Stamp at the De la Pole Hospital during the May 1957 royal visit.

Being presented to the Queen is Miss D. H. Dronfield of Castle Hill Sanatorium. Also pictured are Mr E. Andrew, Mr E. A. Hill, Mr J. E. Stamp, Miss A. Blaney and Dr R. Hardy.

Flags are waved as the Queen leaves a house in Waveney Road, Hull, after paying a surprise visit.

The Queen and Prince Philip reviewing youth organisations in East Park during the royal visit of May 1957.

The Chancellor of Hull University, Lord Middleton, invites the Queen Mother to open the new library on her visit to the city in June 1960.

The Queen Mother talks with Alderman W. E. Body, Lord Mayor of Hull.

Four-year-old Thomas Rippin leads the Queen Mother by the hand into his 'house'.

Almost hidden by flags being waved, the Queen Mother smiles as she leaves the Sailors' Children's Society home at Newland.

Walking through the Newland home, the Queen Mother appears to have a smile for everyone.

Princess Alexandra talking to Mrs J. Watson, chairman of Hull Society for the Mentally Handicapped Children in November 1965. Looking on is Councillor C. W. Hobden.

Princess Alexandra stops for a word with staff at the Holden Centre.

The Duke of Edinburgh talks to Scout canoeists at Sir Leo Schultz High School in June 1967.

The Queen unveils a plaque to mark the opening of Hull Royal Infirmary in June 1967.

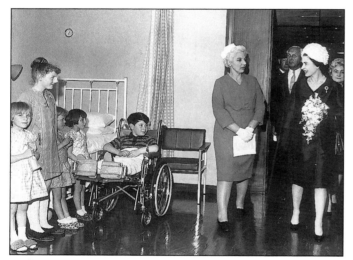

Patients wait nervously as the Queen enters the children's ward at Hull Royal Infirmary.

Mr J. Gambardella escorts the Queen through the infirmary's kitchens.

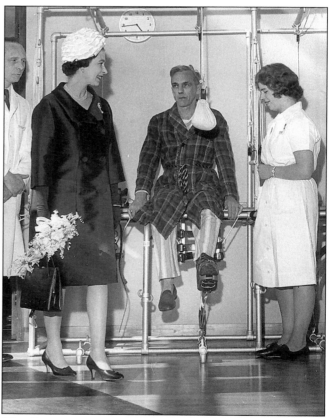

The Queen meets a patient doing physiotherapy during her visit in June 1967.

The Duke of Edinburgh in Hull for the 60th anniversary of the Wildfowlers' Association of Great Britain and Ireland at the Guildhall in July 1968.

The Lord Mayor of Hull invites the Duke to sign the distinguished visitors' book.

Early arrivals wait for a glimpse of the Queen in August 1969.

Prince Edward (left) and Prince Andrew leave Hull's Paragon Station to be driven to the royal yacht *Britannia*, moored at King George Dock.

Crowds line Lowgate as a procession of cars carrying senior members of the royal family passes by in August 1969.

The Lord Mayor's Show

Hull's first Lord Mayor's Show wound its way through the city on 18 May 1968. Traffic was halted and thousands lined the route as a massive convoy of 50 floats, four bands and marchers from civilian organisations passed by.

The show was organised by RAF Partington and the Royal Air Forces Association to mark the RAF's 50th anniversary. Following the procession were two RAF Whirlwind helicopters from Leconfield's 202 Search and Rescue Squad, one flying the RAF Ensign, the other the Union Flag.

The Lord Mayor's Show is now an annual event in Hull.

The first-ever Lord Mayor's Show in Hull passes along George Street towards the city centre in May 1968.

This Blackburn B2 training aircraft, built in 1932, had an honoured place in the 1968 Lord Mayor's Show.

The 1968 Hull Lord Mayor's Show passes down King Edward Street.

This 1968 float illustrated the great changes that had overtaken the Royal Air Force over 50 years.

An RAF band leads the 1968 Lord Mayor's Show through Hull's city centre.

In 1969, the Lord Mayor, accompanied by Mr C. A. Wise, president of Hull Junior Chamber of Commerce and Shipping, has a pat for Beauty, the horse who pulled the mayoral landau.

A selection of transport over the years turns into Jameson Street in 1969.

Girls on the Ideal-Standard float in 1969.

The 150 Northumbrian Regiment, Royal Corps of Transport (V) in the 1969 parade.

Crowds line King Edward Street as the 1970 Lord Mayor's Show passes by.

'Miss Flying Angel' and her retinue on the Missions to Seamen float in 1970.

A vital message is hammered home by Hull City Police's Accident Prevention Department in the 1970 Show.

The Lord Mayor acknowledges crowds in Jameson Street at the 1971 Show.

Girls of the Hawker-Siddeley Aviation Ltd netball team flying high at the 1971 Lord Mayor's Show.

Dressed in 1920s style to ride in a vintage De Large in the 1974 Lord Mayor's Show are these girls from a Hull store.

A veteran engine from Hull Fire Brigade is ready to take part in the 1972 Show.

All the Fun of the Fair

Hull Fair is held each year for a week around 11 October. It fills a site adjacent to Walton Street, west of the city, and is reputed to be the largest travelling fair in England. The fair has been on the present site since 1888. There have been many changes both in the site and the date of the fair and at its foundation in 1278 the fair was probably held outside the walls of a church which stood on the site of the present Holy Trinity Church.

Hull Fair in 1911, showing what today would be called a 'pirate ship'.

Parents wait for their children by the carousel at the 1911 Hull Fair.

Doing their party piece for the *Hull Daily Mail* cameraman in 1931 were these two elephants who appeared there with Bostock and Wombwell. It was the last time that this famous menagerie appeared at Hull Fair.

This young Hull girl sought thrills of a spiral kind as she slides to earth on the helter-skelter at the 1949 Hull Fair.

It doesn't matter how young or old you are, the fun of the fair is just the same. This man and boy enjoy a ride on the carousel in 1953.

The big wheel is in full turn at the 1946 Hull Fair. Just after the end of World War Two, it was not surprising that one attraction (to the right of the picture) should be decorated with heroic pictures of military aircraft.

We'd probably find it rather tasteless today, but in 1953 Hull Fair was where you could see the 'smallest woman', a 'living doll' and Tom Thumb, 'the mighty atom'.

And here are two of the attractions, Titania (left) and Anita. In those less enlightened times ordinary people found little difficulty in paying to see those less fortunate than themselves.

And just to underline the point, here is another group of adults looking after their youngsters… any excuse!

A smile on his face and not a care in the world, that's this Hull youngster at the 1956 Fair.

The twinkling lights make a fairyland by night with the canvas-topped stalls and amusements resembling giant toadstools. This is the 1957 Hull Fair.

A section of the large crowd which watched the Lord Mayor officially open the 1957 Hull Fair.

Mum, dad and youngster all squeeze into a dodgem car at the 1961 Fair.

Saturday-night style at the 1961 Fair as these four young people watch the dodgems.

When she opened the 1972 Hull Fair, the Lady Mayoress met George, at 7ft 3ins reputed to be the tallest man in Scotland.

Early thrills for these youngsters as the 1976 Hull Fair gets under way.

With the Waltzer for his pulpit, the Revd Geoffrey McCulloch, vicar of St Matthew's Church, takes part in the traditional Hull Fair service in 1976. Hessle High School brass band provides the music.

In 1978, members of Hull Amateur Operatic Society found the Fair an ideal promotional vehicle for the forthcoming production. There are no prizes for guessing it was – *Carousel.*

Sporting Hull

Hull City's most famous goalkeeper was Billy Bly, who made 456 League and Cup appearances for the Tigers. Imagine what total he would have achieved but for losing seven seasons to World War Two. He signed for Hull in August 1937 and made his last senior appearance in 1960. He broke many bones during his career, one such injury robbing him of an England 'B' cap.

Chris Chilton In 477 League and Cup games for the Tigers between 1960 and 1971 he scored 222 goals.

Another prolific goalscorer, Ken Wagstaff. Joining the Tigers from Mansfield Town for £40,000 in November 1964, Wagstaff went on to score 197 goals in 434 League and Cup games before injury forced him to retire in January 1975.

Stuart Pearson signed for Hull as a youngster in 1965 but for the first three years combined playing soccer with an apprenticeship at Hull's telephone company. Manchester United paid a Hull record fee of £200,000 for him in May 1974. Pearson won 15 England caps and scored in the 1977 FA Cup Final. He later joined West Ham United.

The next manager of Manchester United? In February 1999, Steve McClaren was head-hunted from Derby County by United boss Alex Ferguson to become his assistant at Old Trafford. McClaren, began his career with the Tigers in 1977 and made over 200 League and Cup appearances for them before being transferred to Derby in July 1985.

Brian Marwood scored 53 goals in 191 League and Cup appearances for Hull City between 1979 and 1984 after signing as an apprentice in 1976. He eventually left for Sheffield Wednesday for £115,000 and then cost Arsenal £600,000 in 1988, the year he won his first England cap. Today he works as a television commentator.

Jim Drake of Hull FC, legend of the awesome Hull pack of the late 1950s and early '60s. He also played for Great Britain.

Bob Coverdale of Hull FC in the 1950s. He skippered Wakefield Trinity and was 'A' team coach to Hull Kingston Rovers.

Skipper Johnny Whiteley, Hull's loose forward, presents Mike Smith – making his debut with the first team at Wembley – to the Duke of Edinburgh before the 1960 Challenge Cup Final.

Bill Drake of Hull FC. Bill, twin brother of Jim Drake, was also a legend of the Hull pack in the late 1950s and early '60s.

A determined Norman Oliver, the Hull winger, goes into a tackle against Lord, his opposite number, during a match against Bradford Northern at the Boulevard in August 1966.

Paul Rose, a 14-year-old Jervis HS prop forward, was chosen for the England Schoolboys RL team to visit France in October 1967. He played for both Hull and Rovers and was a Great Britain international.

John Taylor, one of Hull Kingston Rovers' best finds for many years, pictured in September 1958. He was a Rovers forward.

Alan Burwell, a Hull Kingston Rovers back, played in the 1968 World Cup for Great Britain.

Bryan Tyson of Rovers gets ready for a match in January 1962.

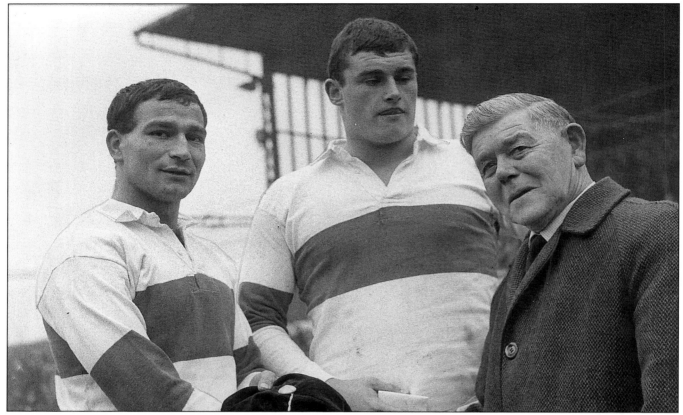

Fred Alford, a member of the Hull KR board, presents Alan Burwell with his county cap and Philip Lowe with his county badge before the start of the Robins' match against Huddersfield at Craven Park in December 1968.

Hull KR's centre and captain, John Moore.

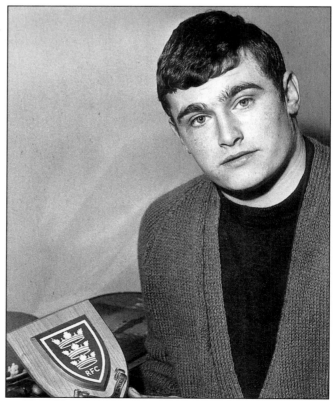

Kingston Rovers' second row forward Phil Lowe pictured after he was selected to tour Australia and New Zealand with the Great Britain party in 1970. He is holding a plaque made for him by a workmate to celebrate his 20th birthday.

Bob Walker, chairman of Hull KR Supporters' Club, presents the 1969 Player of the Year trophy to Phil Lowe. Left to right are Wilf Spavin, Lowe, Walker and new president Percy Johnson.

Peter Flanagan of Hull Kingston Rovers, was a Great Britain International Tourist and was in the Great Britain World Cup squad.

Steve Crooks of Hull Kingston Rovers, played and coached at both Hull and Rovers.

Len Casey of Hull Kingston Rovers with the 1980 Challenge Cup and the 1981 Premiership Trophy.

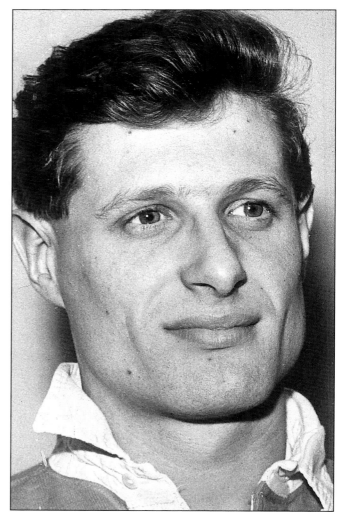

Roger Sangwin, England international and Hull and East Riding RUFC centre, pictured in October 1962.

John Buckton, an England rugby union international.

England Ladies' soccer captain, Carol Thomas from Hull, who played for Reckitts.

Carol Thomas (left) and Flo Bilton, secretary of Hull Women's Football League.

Gail Borman, who played for England.

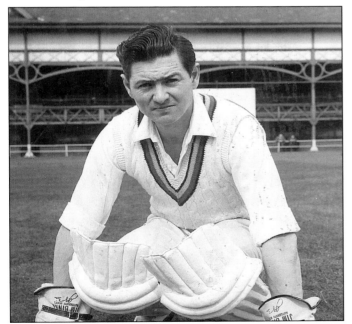

Hull-born Jimmy Binks was Yorkshire's wicketkeeper for 491 first-class matches between 1955 and 1969 and played two Tests for England. From his debut he played in 412 consecutive games before missing a match and his 107 victims in 1960 was a Yorkshire record. In 1972 he became sales manager for Fenners in Hull before emigrating to the USA in 1978.

Bob Piercy of Hull Spartan strides out to retain his half-mile title at Hull and East Riding athletics championships on the Costello track in July 1957.

August 1973 and Dawn Webster regains her Yorkshire womens' 400 metres title, breasting the tape ahead of Christine Howell (No.5, City of Hull). The 1972 champion, Sue Howell (No.11, City of Hull), was in fourth place.

Sixteen-year-old Dawn Webster of Hull Spartan won the Yorkshire womens' 400 metres title and earned the Phyliss Pope Trophy (which she is holding) for the most meritorious performance of the day at Cleckheaton in May 1970.

May 1973 and Malcolm Prince has just smashed Hull Grammar School's 1,500 metres record with a time of 4min 13.8sec. The old record was 4min 41.6sec.

June 1982 and the same Malcolm Prince, now an international athlete of some renown, strides home at the head of the Cottingham race.

Sue Hearnshaw of Hull Spartan competing in the Northern Counties AAA's meeting at the Alderman Kneeshaw track in June 1977.

Sixteen-year-old Malet Lambert schoolboy Dave Smith pictured after a tremendous double hammer-throwing success in the 1978 Northern Under-20 Championships at Stretford. He won gold in both the junior and youth events.

Con O'Kelly became a Roman Catholic priest but this picture shows him as a successful boxer (left) sparring with Detective Miller at Hull in 1937.

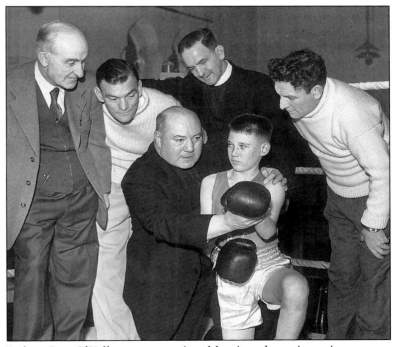

Father Con O'Kelly, once a national boxing champion, gives young Tony Hindley a few tips during St Charles' Boys' Boxing Club training night in St Charles' Street School, Pryme Street, in November 1959. Also in the picture are J. Sheridan, J. Kilkenny, Father J. Knowles and F. Hindle.

Commonwealth Games gold medal boxing champion Roger Tighe shows his medal to neighbours at his mother's home in St George's Road, Hull, in 1966.

Hull heavyweight Roger Tighe gets to close quarters with Bunny Johnson of Jamaica during their fight at the City Hall, Hull, in August 1969. Tighe won on points.

The Lord Mayor of Hull, Councillor L. Johnson, gives three cheers for Hull's champion ABA boxers when he welcomed featherweight Ricky Beaumont (left) and light-heavyweight Malcolm Heath to the Guildhall in May 1975.

Fish Trades' light-heavyweight Malcolm Heath puts Chester-le-Street's Ronnie Nairns on the canvas and went on to win this semi-final bout on points in 1975.

Jackie Turner, a bantamweight with the Fish Trades Amateur Boxing Club. He won two ABA boxing championships and a European bronze.

Alan Peacock takes it on the chin. He boxed for Hull Boys Club and also for England.

Terry Granville, then aged 19, pictured in 1963 with some of the prizes he had won for swimming. He had represented Great Britain in Europe and Australia and held several English butterfly records.

Paula Kilvington, a 17-year-old member of the Avenue Badminton Club, and one of the city's most successful players, pictured in 1974. She was an international player, becoming one of the best badminton players in the country.

May 1968 and young Sally Pickering becomes the first Humbersider to win the Yorkshire women's 110 yards championship since it was first held in 1899.

Sixteen-year-old Sue Edmondson of Hull was ranked an Olympic possible when this photograph was taken in June 1972. She had already become the first British woman to beat 4min 40secs for the 400 metres freestyle in a long course pool. She went on to swim in the Olympic and Commonwealth Games.

Hull's Mike Bailey clambers from the pool after winning the Yorkshire mile championship in 1969, for the fourth successive year.

Jackie Brown, Hull's Olympic international swimmer, pictured in 1972 with some of her recent awards including the Henry Dixon Trophy for Yorkshire's outstanding swimmer of the year.

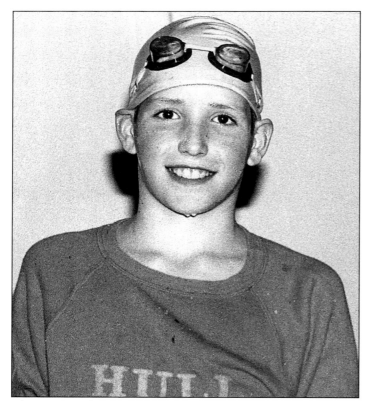

Eleven-year-old Kevin Boyd of Hull Olympic after winning another gold medal at the 1977 North-East Counties Swimming Championships at Hartlepool. He later swam for England.

Hull's famous swimmer Jack Hale, pictured in June 1992 with eight medals which he had recently won at the Crystal Palace.

Famous Faces

The English poet and politician Andrew Marvell (1621-78) was MP for Hull and wrote several poems in praise of Oliver Cromwell as well as powerful satires on the policies of King Charles II.

This lifelike model is of William Wilberforce the great emancipator of slaves, who was born in the High Street, Hull, in 1759.

Local businessman and benefactor Thomas Robinson Ferens left many marks on Hull, not least the Ferens Art Gallery and the Ferensway thoroughfare.

In 1930, Hull's Amy Johnson became the first woman aviator to fly solo from England to Australia, and broke other records on flights to India and Japan (1931), Cape Town (1932) and with her husband to the USA and India (1934). There was even a popular song about her, *Amy, Wonderful Amy*.

Hull-born film director Gerald Thomas, famous for the *Carry On* films among others.

J. Arthur Rank, the founder of the Rank Organisation of cinemas, dance halls and bingo clubs, was born in Hull.

Seated in the director's chair on the set for the film *Conspiracy of Hearts* starring, among others, Lilli Palmer, Sylvia Syms, David Kossoff, Peter Arne and Megs Jenkins, is Hull-born Ralph Thomas.

Hull-born playwright Alan Plater checks a casting directory helped by his children Janet and Stephen in 1968.

Brian Rix, a native of Hull, pictured during the time he was appearing in *Let Sleeping Wives Lie* at the London's New Theatre in 1969. Most famous for the 'Whitehall Farces', he later retired from acting to lead a mental health charity and was knighted.

We perhaps best remember him as Bertie Wooster. In real life, Ian Carmichael tends flowers in the garden of his Ferriby home in October 1956.

Hull actor Barry Rutter enjoys a drink with his grandmother Mrs S. Dixon before he goes out to bat in a charity cricket match in September 1974. He is now a respected director in theatre.

Tom Courtenay visited his native city of Hull for the showing of his film *The Loneliness of the Long Distance Runner*.

Norman Collier of Hull, renowned for his cockerel imitation, tries to tell the old joke during a visit to a Yorkshire turkey farm at Christmas 1972.

Hull's Roy North with the trendiest fox on TV, Basil Brush, in 1973.

Sheila Mercer (*Emmerdale's* Annie Sugden) returned to her native East Coast in 1987 to open the new Tay Homes development in Alexandra Drive, Bridlington.

It's hard to imagine that this is Hull-born actress and comedian Maureen Lipman, but the photograph was taken over 30 years ago.

Home in Hull for a few days after having his tonsils removed is David Whitfield, who in the 1950s was a singing star and 'housewives' heartthrob'. He is pictured helping his elder son Lance with a model train set. He appeared at the Royal Variety Performance and had many hit records.

Glam rocker from the 1970s – Hull guitarist, Mick Ronson, who died in April 1993. He played with David Bowie's backing band and formed a recording partnership with Ian Hunter from Mott The Hoople. His last recording was entitled *Heaven and Hull*.

It's a long way from Greatfield. Hull-born new wave singing star Lene Lovich (left), and pictured in her schooldays (above). She had a top five hit record with *Lucky Number* in 1979.

Hull entertainer Joe Longthorne, pictured here in 1975 with his personal secretary Christine Dunn.

And finally… Although not a native of Hull, Arthur Lucan – 'Old Mother Riley' – found his final resting place in the city's Eastern Cemetery.

Days on the Parks

Park keeper and small children alike are fascinated by the appearance of a cameraman at Pearson Park around the turn of the century.

Crowds throng Pearson Park on the day of King George V's coronation in 1911.

Art students at work in Pearson Park between the wars.

Mothers and children admire the floral clock at Pearson Park after World War Two.

Trainee gardener Micheal O'Brien works in the new garden at Pearson Park in July 1957.

The Old Town Hall Tower in Pearson Park, pictured in May 1958.

A fine display of blooms in the Pearson Park Conservatory in May 1958.

The good old days? The caption which accompanied this August 1960 photograph of Pearson Park read: 'A peaceful spot during the day, but at night a meeting point for rowdies. Even in daylight, dirt-track riders and learner-drivers make the residents of Kingston Villa Old People's Home frightened to cross the road.'

All is quiet on the lake in Pearson Park now that the children are back at school in September 1958.

The imposing entrance to Pearson Park, outlined against a spring sky in 1962.

This gentleman enjoyed his sandwich in the shade at Pearson Park in June 1975, at the start of one of the hottest summers on record. The following year was also a scorcher.

Pickering Park

The pond and shrubbery in Pickering Park in 1949. The *Hull Daily Mail* said that 'this summer … many visitors have commented favourably upon it.'

In 1954, the park keeper at Pickering Park, Mr K. Sanderson, started with six pairs of budgerigars in the park's aviary. When this photograph was taken in 1957 he had over 100.

David Wilkinson is looking after the spring blooms in the Pickering Park Conservatory in March 1960.

Pickering Park's golden jubilee in 1961 was marked by this floral trawler.

Cloistered calm in Pickering Park in March 1969, yet the man reading the newspaper is only a few steps from a busy highway.

Corky, the grass monkey, with Mr A. Major, one of the staff at Pickering Park in July 1969.

Schoolchildren enjoying the 1970 summer holiday break in Pickering Park.

Keeping cool in the Pickering Park paddling pool in the hot summer of 1976.

West Park

Well-dressed ladies and gentlemen leave West Park around the turn of the century.

The Bandstand at West Park, photographed probably in Edwardian times.

Hull youngsters enjoy the paddling pool at West Park in July 1961.

By contrast, a Christmas card view of West Park in March 1970.

Two months later, in May 1971, and in glorious spring sunshine these Hull citizens can enjoy a game of bowls at West Park.

The Anlaby Road entrance to West Park pictured in July 1972.

Music on a midsummer's evening in 1974 as the Hunsley Beacon Orchestra draw a large audience to their concert in West Park.

Paul and David Sugden and William Rahtz keep cool in the West Park pool in June 1981.

East Park

The remains of the gaol in East Park, pictured in October 1946.

Racing underway in the National Dock Labour Board Regatta held at East Park in May 1956.

Dennis Green attracts an audience as he tries out his remote-controlled motor launch in the East Park model pond in May 1958.

Youngsters pose by the drinking fountain in East Park on a hot summer's day, probably in the late 1950s.

Hundreds of people turned out to see the circus elephants parade from Paragon Station to East Park in August 1968.

A new swing is a big attraction in East Park in April 1969.

These boys completed their boat switching without incident on the East Park boating lake in April 1969, but it would have made the organisers of the local water safety week shudder.

A summer Saturday in East Park in July 1969.

Those lazy, hazy days of summer… two people fishing, one just thinking… East Park in July 1976.

In May 1976 the slush boat in East Park proved an ever-popular attraction.

Children play happily around the only remaining relic of the old Hull Citadel, commonly once known as the Garrison. This watch tower, which once stood proudly at the junction of the Hull and Humber Rivers, was still an interesting landmark when this photograph was taken in July 1976.

Out and About

Toll Gravel, Beverley, pictured at the turn of the century.

Youngsters line up against the wall in Butcher Row, Beverley, in the 1890s.

Brough's grocery shop in Cross Street, Beverley, on a site later occupied by Pottage Brothers, ironmongers.

Beverley's Market Cross, pictured after World War Two.

The architectural gem of the East Riding – Beverley Minster floodlit in 1953.

Dr Ivan Hall of Hengate, Beverley, took this photograph to illustrate the traffic problem on what was a major road through the town.

A picture of the Wednesday Market, Beverley, looking towards Butcher Row in May 1961.

Cottingham

Hallgate looking towards St Mary's Church, Cottingham, around the turn of the century.

Beck Bank, Cottingham, on a December day in 1962.

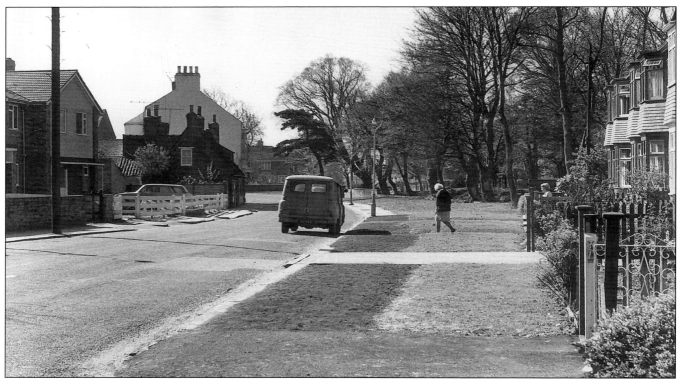

Another view of Beck Bank, in May 1967.

Ye Olde Blue Bell public house in Cottingham.

This truly rural view was photographed in March 1969 but was surrounded by dwellings in residential Cottingham, at the junction of Eppleworth Road and Dene Road.

Snuff Mill House, Cottingham, a charming building with a truly distinctive style.

Hedon

A turn-of-the-century view of Hedon with St Augustine's Church towering majestically over Souttergate.

Hedon army camp in the summer of 1948, still spick and span in military style.

A September day in 1948 and 'Upper', the sole survivor of the magnificent row of elms on the Hull-Witherensea road, is being felled at the corner of Fletcher Gate, Hedon.

July 1961 view of Holywood House, home for senior citizens, and the Kilnsea Cross.

The Painter Cottages at Souttergate, Hedon, in January 1964.

The Market Square, Hedon, in May 1965 with St Augustine's Church in the background.

Hessle

There was some dispute in November 1959 when it was announced that the overhanging branches of these trees in Woodfield Lane, Hessle, were to be cut back to allow buses to pass.

Late autumn day in Davenport Avenue, Hessle, in 1960.

A pastoral scene at Hessle in the late 1960s. It was hard to imagine that the city and port of Hull were just about five miles down the road.

Summer scene in Nordingate, Hessle, in June 1970.

June 1981 and the Humber Bridge is opened. This is the Hessle side.

Willerby

Up for sale – Willerby Railway Station in June 1966.

Aston Road, Willerby, in December 1968. The scene is a tranquil one but only a short distance away in either direction are busy roads leading into the city.

Motorcyclist drives under an archway of green in Great Gutter Lane, Willerby, in May 1970.

The De la Pole Hospital at Willerby in November 1982.

A dog and his master take a walk along Willerby Low Road in January 1969.

Willerby's Cottage Cheese public house